눈꽃 아가
Snow Flower Songs

이해인 영문시집

눈꽃 아가

Claudia Hae In Lee's Lyrics of Nature
SNOW FLOWER SONGS

김진섭 · 유진 W. 자일펠더 옮김

새로 쓰는 시인의 말

 첫 시집 『민들레의 영토』를 세상에 내놓은 지 어느덧 반세기 수도원에 입회한 지 61년이 되는 올해, 다시 『눈꽃 아가』를 손에 들고 겸허히 고개 숙여 독자 여러분께 인사를 드립니다.
 그 긴 여정 속에서 시는 언제나 하느님을 향한 저의 기도였고, 세상과 이웃을 향한 사랑의 편지였습니다. 바쁘고 힘든 일상의 삶 속에서도 제 시집을 읽어주신 독자들의 그 따뜻한 마음 덕분에, 오늘도 저는 작은 꽃씨 하나를 심듯이 시를 씁니다.
 『눈꽃 아가』는 그런 제 시의 결 한 자락을 담아 조심스레 꽃피운 책이었습니다.
 자연과 고독, 사랑과 기도, 그 모든 것 속에 숨은 은총의 빛을 담고자 애썼던 저의 진심이 깃든 시집입니다. 이제 이렇게 새로운 모습으로 한국어와 영어로 다시 세상에 나아가게 되니 기쁘고 감사한 마음입니다.
 특히 이 영문시집은, 제 작은 시들이 언어의 벽을 넘어 더 많은 이들과 마음을 나눌 수 있는 귀한 다리가 되어주리라 믿고 싶습니다. 이 번역이 낯선 이들의 마음에도 잔잔한 울림을 전할 수 있기를 그래서 새로운 시의 벗이 생길 수 있길 감히 소망해봅니다.

새롭게 이 시집을 펼치는 젊은 세대의 독자들에게 『눈꽃 아가』는 잠시 멈추어 자신을 들여다보고, 고요한 기쁨을 발견하는 작은 창문이 되었으면 좋겠습니다. 그리고 오래전부터 함께해주신 독자들께는 이 책이 지난 기억을 다시 안아보는 따뜻한 사랑의 인사가 되기를 바랍니다.

눈은 이내 녹지만, 그 순결한 흔적은 마음속에 오래 남습니다. 이 시집이 그런 눈꽃의 자취처럼 삶의 어느 날 어느 순간 당신에게 조용히 다가가 작은 위로가 되기를 바랍니다.

저의 시를 정성껏 번역해주신 김진섭 선생님과 진 자일펠더 신부님께 깊은 감사를 드립니다.

2025년 초여름 부산 광안리 성베네딕도 수녀원에서
이해인 클라우디아 수녀

A New Author's Preface

It has already been half a century since I published my first poetry collection, Dandelion's Turf, and this year marks the 61st year since I entered the monastery. Now, with Snow Flower Songs in my hands, I humbly bow my head and greet you, dear readers, once again.

Throughout that long journey, poetry has always been my prayer to God and a letter of love to the world and to my neighbors. Even in the midst of busy and difficult daily life, it is thanks to the warm hearts of readers who have read my books that I continue to write poems—just as one might gently plant a tiny flower seed.

Snow Flower Songs is a book that carefully carries a small thread of the texture of my poetry. It is filled with my sincere heart, born of my desire to reflect the light of grace hidden within nature and solitude, love and prayer, and all the spaces in between. I am both happy and grateful that this collection now re-emerges into the world in this new form, in both Korean and English.

I especially hope this English edition becomes a precious bridge, allowing my humble poems to cross the barrier of language and reach the hearts of more people. I dare to wish that this translation might offer a quiet resonance, even to those unfamiliar with my language, and that it might help create new companions for poetry.

To young readers who newly open this collection, I hope Snow Flower Songs becomes a small window—one through which they can pause, look inward, and discover the quiet joy that lies within. And to the longtime readers who have accompanied me on this journey, I hope this book serves as a warm greeting of love that gently embraces the memories we have shared.

Though snow melts quickly, its pure traces linger long in the heart. I hope this collection, like the fading footprints of a snowflower, may quietly come to you one day and become a small comfort.

I offer my heartfelt thanks to Mr. Jinsup Kim and

Fr. Gene Zeilfelder for their devoted and careful translation of my poems.

> Early Summer 2025
> St. Benedict Monastery, Gwangalli, Busan
> Sr. Claudia Lee Hae-in

시인의 말

어린 시절부터 시는 나에게 가장 순결하고 애틋한 그리움의 표현이었다.

초등학교 시절 날마다 노래를 부르듯이 시를 낭송하는 가족들 사이에서 가끔은 동요도 지어보며 행복했던 나는 시가 무엇인지도 잘 모르면서 막연히 아름답고 시적인 삶을 꿈꾸곤 했다.

중학교에 들어가 문예반 활동을 했고, 여고시절엔 여러 백일장에서 입상하며 선생님들의 인정과 격려를 받는 일이 기뻤다. 그러나 수도생활을 시작하면서부터는 일단 문학을 포기해야 한다고 생각했기에 가끔 혼자만의 노트에 글을 적어두곤 할 뿐 작품집까지 내며 발표하려는 의도는 없었다. 그러다가 1976년 종신서원을 전후로 당시의 수도원 원장님이 한국의 어느 원로시인에게 그동안 써 모은 나의 시들을 한 번 보이게 했고, 그 시인이 혼자 보기 아깝다며 출판을 간곡히 권유한 것이 계기가 되어 첫 시집 『민들레의 영토』가 세상에 빛을 보게 되었다. 그 이후로 틈틈이 시를 발표하였고, 2006년이면 첫 시집이 나온 지 30주년이 된다.

나의 시는 바로 나 자신에게, 이웃에게, 신神에게 그리고 자연과 사물에게 보내는 진솔하고 겸허한 사랑의 편지라고 생각된다.

내가 쓰는 시의 주제들은 자연, 사랑, 고독, 기도로 구분할 수 있을 것 같고 일부 평자가 말하는 것처럼 어떤 큰 철학이나 사상보다는 '사소하고 무상한 사물이나 인정을 불멸과 무한, 즉 영원 속에다 연결하려는 노력'인지도 모르겠다.

어쨌든 크게 자랑할 만한 것은 못 되지만 꾸밈없고 소박한 이 마음의 노래들을 지난 30년간 꾸준히 읽어주는 독자들이 많아서 행복하다. 시집을 펴낼 때마다 시를 읽고 보내오는 독자들의 아름다운 편지들을 나는 버리지 않고 모아두었다. 사연도 가지각색인 독자들의 수많은 편지들은 세상과 수도원을 이어주는 다리 역할을 해주며 때로는 내가 쓰는 시들의 소재가 되기도 한다.

하루에 적어도 네 번 시편으로 만든 성무일도를 바칠 때마다 나는 누구보다도 시적인 삶을 살고 있다고 생각되며, 고독과 침묵의 수도생활을 통해서 나 자신도 조금씩 '버릴 것은 버리고' 한 편의 시가 되어가는 느낌을 받는다.

김진섭 선생님과 진 자일펠더 신부님의 정성스런 영역을 통해 이제 나의 작은 노래들이 해외의 독자들에게도

읽혀질 것을 생각하면 기쁘고 설레는 마음 가득하다. 이런 기회를 허락해준 열림원 출판사와 편집진들께도 감사드린다.

　앞으로도 나는 시라는 창문을 통해 세상을 보고 이웃을 이해하고 신을 섬기며 일생을 헌신하는 한 송이의 민들레가 되리라. 내가 사는 민들레의 영토, 민들레의 바다에서 나는 늘 잠들면서도 깨어 있는 사랑의 시인, 사랑의 구도자가 되고 싶다.

2005년 10월

이해인

Author's Preface

Since childhood, poetry has been a genuine expression of my ardent yearning. When I was in elementary school, without much understanding of poetry, I occasionally used to compose a few verses to present to my family as the members routinely recited some poems. And I dreamed of an indefinably beautiful poetic life. Being involved in literary circles while attending high school, I was delighted to be recognized by my teachers as I won several prizes in local composition contests.

Commencing my religious life, I decided to discontinue writing poems for public release but casually jotted them down in my notebook. When I made my final profession in 1976, Mother Superior, recognizing my poetry, strongly urged me to resume my poetry work and to share my talent with others even though I initially hesitated to do so. She also recommended me to a senior poet who highly valued my poetry and greatly assisted me in having my first anthology, Dandelion's Turf, presented to readers. Since then, I have written poems from time to time and released them to the public. Next year, I will commemorate the thirtieth anniversary of the first book.

For me, writing a poem is a kind of a sincere humble love letter addressed to myself, my neighbors, God and nature. The themes of my poems can be categorized into four areas: love, nature, loneliness and prayer. My poetry might not reflect a great philosophy or depth of thought — as some critics have commented. However, I think it is an effort in bridging futile trivialities and simple humanity to imperishable infinity or eternity.

Although I do not try to boast of my works, I am always happy with readers who have appreciated those songs of my humble heart over the decades. Treasuring all the readers' letters from various walks of life that bridge my religious community to the mundane world, I often have them serve as raw material for my creative work. And reciting the Daily Offices four times a day, I enjoy an ever poetic life and also feel as if I myself were a poem in solitude and silence amidst communal life, shedding things uncritical.

As my plain songs can now globally reach international readers through careful translation by Mr. Jinsup Kim and Fr. Gene Zeilfelder, I am so happy and my heart is overwhelmed. And, for such a precious opportunity, I also wish to extend my sincere gratitude to the publisher, Yolimwon, and its editorial staff.

I desire to see the world, understand my neighbors and serve God as dedicated through the window of poetry, remaining as a dandelion that seeks to be a poet of love in the dandelion's turf as well as one who is ever awake while asleep at the sea of the dandelion.

Sr. Claudia Hae In Lee, OSB

October 2005

Contents

새로 쓰는 시인의 말 A New Author's Preface | 5

시인의 말 Author's Preface | 10

자연
NATURE

가을 산은 The Autumn Mountain | 24

겨울나무 A Winter Tree Speaks | 28

별을 보면 Looking at the Stars | 32

가을 저녁 An Autumn Evening | 38

오늘은 내가 반달로 떠도 Though I Rise as a Half Moon Today | 40

보름달에게 1 To the Full Moon 1 | 44

유월 숲에는 In the Forest of June | 47

풀꽃의 노래 A Grass Flower's Song | 51

잎사귀 명상 Meditating on a Tree's Leaves | 55

나무의 자장가 A Tree's Lullaby | 59

꽃 한 송이 되어 A Paulownia Beckons Me | 63

물망초 Forget Me Not | 67

해 질 녘의 단상 Fragmentary Thoughts at Sunset | 69

숲에서 쓰는 편지 Letters I Write in the Forest | 84

풀물 든 가슴으로 A Grass-Tinged Heart | 90

사랑
LOVE

민들레의 영토 Dandelion's Turf | 96

해바라기 연가 A Sunflower's Love Song | 102

나비의 연가 A Butterfly's Love Song | 106

사랑에 대한 단상 Fragmentary Thoughts on Love | 111

봉숭아 A Touch-me-not | 117

석류꽃 A Pomegranate Blossom | 119

호박꽃 A Pumpkin Flower | 121

사랑도 나무처럼 The Changing Look of Love | 123

다른 옷은 입을 수가 없네 No New Wardrobe | 127

소녀들에게 To the Girls | 129

상사화 A Lovesick Flower | 135

파도의 말 A Wave Speaks | 139

석류의 말 A Pomegranate's Words | 141

동백꽃이 질 때 When a Camellia Falls | 144

찔레꽃 A White Wild Rose | 148

고독
LONELINESS

11월에 In November | 156

진달래 O Azalea | 160

파도여 당신은 You, O Wave | 164

사랑 Love | 168

바람이여 You, O Wind | 172

나무의 마음으로 With a Tree's Heart | 176

나목 일기 A Naked Tree's Diary | 180

선인장 O Cactus | 184

비 오는 날의 일기 A Rainy Day's Diary | 188

장미를 생각하며 Reflecting on a Rose | 198

너에게 가겠다 I Will Come to You | 202

이끼 낀 돌층계에서 On the Mossy Stone Steps | 206

사르비아의 노래 A Salvia's Song | 209

어느 조가비의 노래 A Shell's Song | 213

해 질 무렵 어느 날 At Sunset on a Certain Day | 218

기도
PRAYER

장미의 기도 A Rose's Prayer | 226

다시 바다에서 At the Sea Again | 230

한 송이 수련으로 Desiring to be a Water Lily | 234

엉겅퀴의 기도 A Thistle's Prayer | 238

꽃밭에 서면 Standing in the Flower Garden | 243

제비꽃 연가 A Violet's Love Song | 247

겨울 아가 1 Winter Song of Songs 1 | 251

가난한 새의 기도 A Poor Bird's Prayer | 255

눈꽃 아가 Snow Flower Songs | 259

봄까치꽃 A Magpie Flower in Spring | 269

춘분 일기 Diary on the Vernal Equinox | 273

외딴 마을의 빈집이 되고 싶다 Longing to be Empty and Isolated | 277

작은 위로 Small Comfort | 279

능소화 연가 A Trumpet Vine's Love Song | 283

아침의 향기 The Fragrance of Morning | 286

자연
NATURE

―――

산길을 돌며 예전에 심은 메타세쿼이아 나무가

너무 빨리 커버린 것을 바라보며 감회가 깊습니다.

나무는 나에게 늘 시를 주고 싶어합니다.

내가 심은 나무가 더 커서 나를 내려다보는 아침.

나는 문득 그와 헤어질 어느 날을 생각하며 나직이 묻습니다.

"내가 죽으면 네 옆에 묻힐까?"

"글쎄……."

왠지 곤란한 듯 선뜻 대답을 못 하는 나의 나무.

나무들 사이로 보이는 태양이 오늘따라 눈부셨어요.

나도 힘차게 일어서야지.

나도 하늘을 향해 올라가야지.

―――

Walking along the mountain pass, I casually observe the dawn redwood I planted long ago. The tree always seems to desire to hand me a poem. It has grown so fast and is now taller than I am. Thus the tree I once planted looks down on me this morning, and it makes me deeply sentimental. Suddenly reminding myself that I must depart, I ask the tree in a low voice, "Will I be buried beside you?"

"Well……." Being somehow embarrassed, it doesn't immediately respond. And today, the sun shining with unusual brilliance through the trees dazzles me. I will arise powerfully and go up toward the sky.

가을 산은

가을 산은
내게 더 가까이 있고
더 푸르게 있다

슬픔 가운데도 빛나는
내 귀한 연륜

시시로
높은 산정 오르며
생각했지

눈 감으면 보이고
눈 뜨면 사라지는
나의 사랑

하 그리 고운 언어들
많이도 잊었지만
은총의 빛 얻어

슬프지 않은

가을날
희게 손을 씻고 뛰어가는
당신의 언덕길

덧없이 숨이 차옴은
그게 다 어린 탓이라고
혼자 생각에

마음 더욱
가난히 키워
고개를 들면

가을 산은
내게 더 가까이 있고
더 푸르게 있다

The Autumn Mountain

With deepening verdure

The autumn mountain

Is ever nearer to me.

Even in sorrow

My precious annual growth ring glows.

From time to time

Climbing the mountain top,

I reflect—

It is my love

That appears in my sight with eyes closed

And disappears therefrom with eyes open.

Into oblivion

My countless refined words sink.

Yet, enlightened by grace,

I am not saddened.

On that autumn day
I run to your hillcrest
With my hands washed clean.

Becoming breathless all too soon,
I blame my childish thinking only.

As my heart grows poorer
I raise my head.

Then, with deepening verdure
The autumn mountain
Is ever nearer to me.

겨울나무

내 목숨 이어가는
참 고운 하늘을
먹었습니다

눈 감아도 트여오는
백설의 겨울 산길
깊숙이 묻어둔
사랑의 불씨

감사하고 있습니다
살아온 날
살아갈 날
넘치는 은혜의 바다

사랑하고 있습니다
가는 세월
오는 세월
기도하며 지새운 밤

종소리 안으로
밝아오는 새벽이면
영원을 보는 마음

해를 기다립니다
내 목숨 이어가는
너무 고운 하늘을
먹었습니다

A Winter Tree Speaks

I have absorbed the splendid sky
That sustains my life.

Even closing my eyes,
I see a path opening
Along the snow covered
Winter mountain.
Yet the ember of love remains
Deeply concealed within.

I am grateful
For the days I have lived
And for those I shall live
In the sea of full grace.

I love those days going by,
Those coming forth,
And those nights I sit up in prayer.

With the bell tolling

As day breaks

My heart sees

The eternity within.

I look forward to the sun's rising.

I have absorbed the splendid sky

That sustains my life.

별을 보면

하늘은
별들의 꽃밭

별을 보면
내 마음
뜨겁게 가난해지네

내 작은 몸이
무거워
울고 싶을 때

그 넓은 꽃밭에 앉아
영혼의 호흡 소리
음악을 듣네

기도는 물
마실수록 가득 찬 기쁨

내일을 약속하는
커단 거울 앞에
꿇어 앉으면

안으로 넘치는 강이
바다가 되네
길은 멀고 아득하여
피리 소린 아직도
끝나지 않았는데

별 뜨고
구름 가면
세월도 가네

오늘은 어제보다
죽음이
한 치 더 가까워도

평화로이
별을 보며
웃어주는 마음

훗날
별만이 아는 나의 이야기
꽃으로 피게

살아서 오늘을 더 높이
내 불던 피리
찾아야겠네

Looking at the Stars

The sky is a flower garden of the stars.

As I look at the stars,
My heart turns hot and poor.

As heavy is my tiny body,
I feel like crying.

Then, I sit in the vast flower garden,
Listening to the music
Of a soul breathing.

Prayer seems to be like water—
The more I drink,
The more my joy overflows.

I kneel before the big mirror
That promises my tomorrow.

The river overflowing within

Turns into the sea.

My way is long and distant

And the sound of fiddling has not yet ended.

Still time and tide flow

As the stars rise and the clouds flow.

Today, death inches closer to me

Than it did yesterday.

Peacefully,

I look at the stars,

Wearing a big smile

In my heart.

As known to the stars,

I desire my story

To come to flower someday.

And I shall seek the fiddle I used to play,

Making today more exalted while living.

가을 저녁

박하 내음의 정결한 고독의 집
연기가 피네

당신 생각 하나에
안방을 비질하다
한 장의 홍엽紅葉으로
내가 물든 가을 저녁

낡고 정든 신도 벗고
떠나고 싶네

An Autumn Evening

From the lone house
Peppermint scented smoke rises.

In the autumn evening
While sweeping the living room,
I become a red-tinged leaf.

I wish to depart barefoot,
Leaving my fond but worn-out shoes behind.

오늘은 내가 반달로 떠도

손 시린 나목의 가지 끝에
홀로 앉은 바람 같은
목숨의 빛깔

그대의 빈 하늘 위에
오늘은 내가 반달로 떠도
차오르는 빛

구름에 숨어서도
웃음 잃지 않는
누이처럼 부드러운 달빛이 된다

잎새 하나 남지 않은
나의 뜨락엔 바람이 차고
마음엔 불이 붙는 겨울날

빛이 있어
혼자서도

풍요로워라

맑고 높이 사는 법을
빛으로 출렁이는
겨울 반달이여

Though I Rise as a Half Moon Today

Life is tinged by the wind
Standing like the solitary tip of a frozen branch
That hangs on a naked tree.

Though I rise as a half moon today
In your empty sky,
My light shall grow ever brighter.

Even hiding in the clouds,
The moonlight becomes
A tender sister wearing an eternal smile.

In my courtyard
As it's filled with the cold wind
Not a leaf remains.
Yet my heart burns
On this winter day.

Although it appears lonely,
The moon remains rich
With its ever-present light.

You, O waning winter moon,
Your light, so high and clear,
Ripples earthward.

보름달에게 1

너는
나만의 것은 아니면서
모든 이의 것
모든 이의 것이면서
나만의 것

만지면
물소리가 날 것 같은
너

세상엔 이렇듯
흠도 티도 없는 아름다움이 있음을
비로소 너를 보고 안다
달이여

내가 살아서
너를 보는 날들이
얼마만큼이나 될까?

To the Full Moon 1

You are possessed

Not by me alone

But by all.

Yet while you are everyone's,

You remain mine.

Your face is quiet.

Yet reaching out to you

I detect ripples

Lapping at the edges.

In you, O moon,

I've come to see

Flawless beauty

In this world.

Let me count the days

That I still may see you

In this life.

유월 숲에는

초록의 희망을 이고
숲으로 들어가면

뻐꾹새
새 모습은 아니 보이고
노래 먼저 들려오네

아카시아꽃
꽃 모습은 아니 보이고
향기 먼저 날아오네

나의 사랑도 그렇게
모습은 아니 보이고

늘
먼저 와서
나를 기다리네

눈부신 초록의
노래처럼
향기처럼

나도
새로이 태어나네

유월의 숲에 서면
더 멀리 나를 보내기 위해
더 가까이 나를 부르는 당신

In the Forest of June

I walk into the forest
Embracing the green hope.

Even before I'm aware of it
A cuckoo sings its song.

Even before I'm aware of it
An acacia emits its fragrance.

Even before I'm aware of it
Love is there waiting for me.

As the green hope dazzles,
And the fragrance stimulates,
So shall I be born anew.

As I stand in the forest of June
You call me ever nearer

To send me

To a more distant place.

풀꽃의 노래

나는 늘
떠나면서 살지

굳이
이름을 불러주지 않아도 좋아

바람이 날 데려가는 곳이라면
어디서나 새롭게 태어날 수 있어

하고 싶은 모든 말들
아껴둘 때마다
씨앗으로 영그는 소리를 듣지

너무 작게 숨어 있다고
불완전한 것은 아니야
내게도 고운 이름이 있음을
사람들은 모르지만
서운하지 않아

기다리는 법을
노래하는 법을
오래전부터
바람에게 배웠기에
기쁘게 살 뿐이야

푸름에 물든 삶이기에
잊혀지는 것은
두렵지 않아

나는 늘
떠나면서 살지

A Grass Flower's* Song

I live prepared to leave.

You may not necessarily call my name,
I don't mind.

Wherever the wind carries me,
I shall be born anew.

Whenever I hold onto all the words
I want to utter,
I hear them bursting into seeds.

In my concealment
I'm so small,
Yet I'm not incomplete.
Though my pretty name is unknown to people,
I'm not dismayed.

Long ago,

I learned from the wind

How to wait

And how to sing.

So I simply live joyfully.

As my life is dyed green

I never fear being forgotten.

I live prepared to leave.

---

* "Grass Flower" is not a proper noun but rather refers to any of the numerous small, dainty flowers that randomly appear in patches of grass.

잎사귀 명상

꽃이 지고 나면
비로소 잎사귀가 보인다
잎 가장자리 모양도
잎맥의 모양도
꽃보다 아름다운
시詩가 되어 살아온다

둥글게 길쭉하게
뾰족하게 넙적하게

내가 사귄 사람들의
서로 다른 얼굴이
나무 위에서 웃고 있다

마주나기잎
어긋나기잎
돌려나기잎
무리지어나기잎

내가 사랑한 사람들의
서로 다른 운명이
삶의 나무 위에 무성하다

Meditating on a Tree's Leaves

As the flower petals fall
The leaves present themselves.

Even their veins and their shapes
Arise as beautiful poems—
More beautiful than the flowers.

Some are round or oblong,
And some pointed or blunt.

I see those I've met—
Each with a different face,
Smiling over the tree.

Leaves that sprout opposite each other,
Leaves that sprout diagonally from each other,
Leaves that sprout around each other,
And those that sprout in clusters.

I see those I've loved—

Each with a different destiny,

Hanging thickly over the tree.

나무의 자장가

아무리 잠을 청해도
잠이 오지 않는
나른한 여름

눈을 감아도
몸과 마음이
모아지지 않고
멋대로 흩어지는 오후

다디단 바람이 와서
가만가만 나를 달래며
잠들게 해줍니다
초록빛 나뭇잎들이
나무에서 내려와
자장가를 불러줍니다

나는 금방
초록빛 시원한

잠의 숲속으로 들어가
깨어날 줄을 모릅니다

A Tree's Lullaby

In the slack summertime
Languid as I am,
Hardly can I go to sleep
Despite the urgency for rest.

In this afternoon
Though closing my eyes,
I can hardly concentrate
My mind and body—
They slip apart from each other
As they please.

Approaching so sweetly,
Gentle breezes caress me tenderly,
Soothingly making me to fall asleep.
And, descending from the tree,
Green leaves lullaby me—
Lifting me immediately

Into the cool green forest of sleep,

Never do I want to awaken.

꽃 한 송이 되어

비 오는 날
오동꽃이 보랏빛 우산을 쓰고
나에게 말했습니다

넓어져라
높아져라

더 넓게
더 높게 살려면
향기가 없어도 괜찮다

나는 얼른
꽃 한 송이 되어
올라갔습니다

처음으로 올라가본
오동나무의 집은
하도 편안해

내려오고 싶지 않았습니다

당신도 오실래요?

A Paulownia Beckons Me

On a rainy day
Under a violet umbrella
A paulownia flower said to me—

"Inflate yourself
And raise yourself.

Live more expansively
And loftier,
Even without fragrance."

Why don't you join me up here?

Immediately,
I became a flower
And ascended the tree.

Ascending the Paulownia's shelter,

For the first time,

I found it so comfortable

That I didn't want to descend.

물망초

오직
나를 위해서만 살아달라고
나를 잊어선 안 된다고
차마 소리내어
부탁하질 못하겠어요

죽는 날까지
당신을 잊지 않겠다고
내가 먼저 약속하는 일이
더 행복해요

당신을 기억하는
생의 모든 순간이
모두가 다
꽃으로 필 거예요
물이 되어 흐를 거예요

당신을 사랑합니다

Forget Me Not

Hardly can I utter
Words begging you
To love me only,
For my sake alone,
And to forget me not.

More blessed would it be
For me to first promise
I will not forget you
Until the day I die.

As long as I remember you
All of my life's moments
Will surely come to flower
And turn into flowing waters.

I love you.

해 질 녘의 단상

1
어려서부터
나는 늘
해 질 녘이 좋았다

분꽃과 달맞이꽃이
오므렸던 꿈들을
바람 속에 펼쳐내는
쓸쓸하고도 황홀한 저녁
나의 꿈도
바람에 흔들리며
꽃피기를 기다렸다

지는 해를 바라보며
눈물이 핑 도는
이별의 슬픔을
아이는 처음으로 배웠다

2
헤어질 때면
"잘 있어, 응" 하던 그대의 말을
오늘은 둥근 해가 떠나며
내게 전하네

새들도 쉬러 가고
사람들은 일터에서
집으로 돌아가는 겸허한 시간
욕심을 버리고 지는 해를 바라보면
문득 아름다운 오늘의 삶
눈물 나도록 힘든 일이 없는 건 아니지만
견디고 싶은 마음이
고마움이 앞서네

누구라도 용서하지 않으면 안 된다고
그래야 내일의 밝은 해를 밝게 볼 수 있다고
지는 해는 넌지시 일러주며 작별 인사를 하네

3
비바람을 견뎌내고
튼튼히 선 한 그루 나무처럼
오늘이란 땅 위에 선 사람도
어쩔 수 없이 슬픔을 견뎌내야
조금씩 철이 드나 보다

사랑하는 이와의 이별을 경험하고
터무니없는 오해도 받고
자신의 모습에 실망도 하면서
어둠의 시간을 보낸 후에야
가볍지 않은 웃음을 웃을 수 있고
다른 이를 이해하는 일도
좀 더 깊이 있게 할 수 있나 보다

4
찬물로 세수하고

수도원 안 정원의 사철나무와 함께
파랗게 깨어나는 겨울 아침

흰 눈 속의 동백꽃을
자주 찾는 동박새처럼
호랑가시나무 열매를
즐겨 먹는다는 붉은 새처럼

나도 이제는
붉은 꽃, 붉은 열매에
피 흘리는 사랑에 사로잡힌
한 마리 가슴 붉은 새인지도 몰라

겨울에도 쉬지 않고
움직이는 기쁨
시들지 않는 노래로
훨훨 날아다니는 겨울새인지도 몰라

5
귀에는 아프나
새길수록 진실인 말

가시 돋쳐 있어도
향기를 숨긴
어느 아픈 말들이
문득 고운 열매로
나를 먹여주는 양식이 됨을
고맙게 깨닫는 긴긴 겨울밤

좋은 말도 아껴 쓰는 지혜를
칭찬을 두려워하는 지혜를
신神께 청하며 촛불을 켜는 겨울밤

아침의 눈부신 말을 준비하는
벅찬 기쁨으로 나는
자면서도 깨어 있네

6
흰 눈 내리는 날
밤새 깨어 있던
겨울나무 한 그루
창을 열고 들어와
내게 말하네

맑게 살려면
가끔은 울어야 하지만
외롭다는 말은
함부로 내뱉지 말라고

사랑하는 일에도
자주 마음이 닫히고
꽁해지는 나에게
나보다 나이 많은 나무가
또 말하네

하늘을 보려면 마음을 넓혀야지
별을 보려면 희망도 높여야지

이름 없는 슬픔의 병으로
퉁퉁 부어 있는 나에게
어느새 연인이 된 나무는
자기도 춥고 아프면서
나를 위로하네

흰 눈 속에
내 죄를 묻고
모든 것을 용서해주겠다고
나의 나무는 또 말하네
참을성이 너무 많아
나를 주눅 들게 하는
겨울 나무 한 그루

Fragmentary Thoughts at Sunset

1

Since childhood
Have I enjoyed the sunset.

In the fascinating serene evening,
With the wind blowing,
The evening primrose and four-o'clocks unfold
Their enclosed dreams.
And even my dreams sway in the breeze
And look forward to flowering.

Gazing at the setting sun,
A child, with tearful eyes,
Realized that painful separation
For the first time.

2

Today the round setting sun passes on
Your words "OK. Good-bye"
Uttered whenever you depart.

In the humble hours
When birds go for rest
And people return home from work,
I gaze at the setting sun
Ridding my mind of mundane desires.
And despite painfully wrestling with tough things,
I suddenly desire to endure
Today's beautiful life
With thankfulness.

Bidding me farewell,
The setting sun casually suggests
"You must forgive whomever you should.

And then you will clearly see the sun

Tomorrow."

3

Like the sturdy tree

That withstands rainstorms,

Those who stand on this land today,

Can grow somewhat mature

Little by little

As they somehow endure their sorrows.

From experiences in

Separation from a beloved one,

Impossible misapprehension from others,

Disappointment with self-image,

And walking in the darkness,

We may be able to smile without rashness

And to profoundly understand others.

4

Together with the spindle tree in the convent garden,
This winter morning awakes in green
After washing its face in cold water.

The Oriental White-eye* often comes
To the camellias in the snow
And the robin loves
To take the thorn bush's fruit.

Such a bleeding love
For the red flowers
As well as for the red fruit
Enchants me
As if I were a robin.

How joyful it is to move without ceasing

Even in the wintertime!

I might be a winter-bird

Fluttering about with ever-spirited songs.

5

Painfully does a word come to the ears;

Truthfully does it come to the heart.

In this long winter night,

I've come to appreciate those words

That sting me while concealing their flavor.

Then suddenly they become savory fruit

And nourish me.

In this winter night,

I enkindle a candle

And ask God for the wisdom

To sparingly utter sweet words

And to humbly apprehend words of praise.

Preparing a splendid word

To utter in the morning,

And filled with brimming joy,

I remain awake

Even while asleep.

6

On a snowy day

A winter tree

That has stayed awake over the night

Comes to me through the window

And says—

"Desiring to sustain a clean life,

You may weep at times,

But never recklessly voice

A word of your loneliness."

Even when in love,

I am often moody and silent,

Closing my heart.

So the tree, of greater age than I,

Again speaks to me—

"When you desire to look up to the heavens,

You expand your heart.

And, when you desire to look up to the stars,

You lift your hope to the highest."

I am sullen from an unknown ailment.

And, despite its own cold and pain,

The tree comforts me

And becomes a love of mine.

Again, the tree speaks—

"Burying your sins in the snow,

I will forgive you."

Thus, the solitary tree in the wintertime

Humbles me by its great fortitude.

* *Indian Zosterop* (Zosterops palpebrosa) – also known as Indian White-eye

숲에서 쓰는 편지

1
기다리다 못해
내가 포기하고 싶었던 희망

힘들고 두려워
다신 시작하지 않으리라
포기했던 사랑

신록의 숲에서
나는 다시 찾고 있네

순결한 웃음으로
멈추지 않는 사랑으로
신(神)과 하나 되고 싶던
여기 초록빛 잎새 하나

어느 날 열매로 익어 떨어질
초록빛 그리움 하나

2
꽃과 이별한 자리마다
열매를 키워가며 행복한
나무들의 숨은 힘

뿌리 깊은 외로움을 견디어냈기에
더욱 높이 뻗어가는 눈부신 생명이여

신록의 숲에 오면
우린 모두 말없는
초록의 사람들이 되네

사랑이 깊을수록
침묵하는 이유를
나무에게 물으며
말없음표 가득한
한 장의 편지를
그대에게 쓰고 싶네

어느새 숲으로 따라와
모든 눈물과 어둠을 말려주는
고마운 햇빛이여

잃었던 노래를 다시 찾은 나는
나무 같은 그대의 음성을
나무 옆에서 듣네

꽃에 가려져도 주눅 들지 않고
늘 당당한 신록의 잎새들
잎새처럼 싱그러운 사랑을
우리도 마침내
삶의 가지 끝에
피워 올려야 한다고……

Letters I Write in the Forest

1

Tired as I was of waiting,
I once sought to abandon hope.

Weary and fearful as I was to act,
I once sought to abandon love.

Now, in the verdant forest,
I seek these anew.

Wherein hangs a green leaf
With a genuine smile
And unceasing love—
Desiring to be one with God.

Wherein hangs also a green bud of yearning
That will someday ripen
And fall as fruit.

2

Separated from the flowers
The trees are happy
Nurturing the fruits thereon.
Ah, what potential they have!

Having endured loneliness deeply rooted,
They dare to reach ever higher.
What a splendid life they have!

Coming to the forest,
We become a green-tinged people,
Saying nothing.

We ask the trees
Why the deeper their love grows,
The more silent they are.
Now, I feel like writing you a letter

Filling it with "……"

Unaware,

The sun comes to the forest after me

And removes all the tears and darkness.

What gratifying sunshine it beams!

Having found the lost songs

By the tree,

I again hear

Your tree-like voice.

Even overshadowed by the flowers,

The verdant leaves are not intimidated

But self-confident.

Like the leaves,

May our love finally rise

From the tips at the end of our life's branches.

풀물 든 가슴으로

보이는 것
들리는 것 모두
풀빛으로 노래로
물드는 봄

겨우내 아팠던 싹들이
웃으며 웃으며 올라오는 봄

봄에는
슬퍼도 울지 마십시오

신발도 신지 않고
뛰어 내려오는
저 푸른 산이 보이시나요?

그 설렘의 산으로
어서 풀물 든 가슴으로
올라가십시오

A Grass-Tinged Heart

In spring,

All things,

Seen and heard are tinged

With grass colors and their songs.

In spring

Buds that pained

Throughout the winter

Sprout

With laughter.

In spring,

Do not cry

Even in sorrow.

You see the green mountain

Running barefoot toward us,

Don't you?

With your grass-tinged heart,

Go quickly to the mountain

That makes your heart throb.

사랑
LOVE

―

마음에 사랑이 넘치면 눈이 밝아집니다. 부정적인 말로
남을 판단하기보다는 긍정적인 말로 남을 이해하려 애쓰게 됩니다.
마음에 사랑이 넘치면 얼굴 표정에도 맑은 웃음이
늘 배경처럼 깔려 있어 만나는 이들을 기쁘게 할 것입니다.
매우 사소한 것일지라도 다른 사람을 배려하고 그를 위해서
열려 있는 사랑의 행동은 그 자체가 아름다운 보석입니다.
찾기만 하면 늘 널려 있는 이 보석을 찾지 못하는 것은
저의 게으름 때문이지요.

———

When love overflows our hearts, our eyes grow clear and we then try to understand others positively rather than judging in negative words. Then even our facial expressions bear a fresh smile yielding a countenance that makes happy those whom we encounter. When we show consideration of others with even the least acts of love, the acts turn into jewels spreading everywhere and to be found when sought.

Simply, I might be too lazy to seek them.

민들레의 영토

기도는 나의 음악
가슴 한복판에 꽂아 놓은
사랑은 단 하나의
성스러운 깃발

태초부터 나의 영토는
좁은 길이었다 해도
고독의 진주를 캐며
내가
꽃으로 피어나야 할 땅

애처로이 쳐다보는
인정의 고움도
나는 싫어

바람이 스쳐가며
노래를 하면
푸른 하늘에게

피리를 불었지

태양에 쫓기어
활활 타다 남은 저녁노을에
저렇게 긴 강이 흐른다

노오란 내 가슴이
하얗게 여위기 전
그이는 오실까

당신의 맑은 눈물
내 땅에 떨어지면
바람에 날려 보낼
기쁨의 꽃씨

흐려오는
세월의 눈시울에
원색의 아픔을 씹는

내 조용한 숨소리

보고 싶은 얼굴이여

Dandelion's Turf

Prayer is my music
And love a sacred banner
Embedded within my heart.

Though my turf eternally lies
But along a narrow path.
It is there that I should gather
Pearls in my loneliness
And come to flower.

Even a pitiful gaze
From a tender heart
Only makes me cringe.

The wind blows by and sings.
And I, like a piper,
Join in, gazing into the azure sky.

With the twilight remaining ablaze,

And driven by the setting sun,

The long river flows afar.

Till my amber heart turns ashen,

I wonder when

He will lift me to his side.

Falling on me

Your pure tears turn into

The flowering seeds of my delight

And fly off in the blowing wind.

As my eyelids grow dim

Over the years

I swallow my primal pains

Breathing quietly.

What a countenance,

I miss you so much!

해바라기 연가

내 생애가 한 번뿐이듯
나의 사랑도
하나입니다

나의 임금이여
폭포처럼 쏟아져 오는 그리움에
목메어
죽을 것만 같은 열병을 앓습니다

당신 아닌 누구도
치유할 수 없는
내 불치의 병은
사랑

이 가슴 안에서
올올이 뽑은 고운 실로
당신의 비단옷을 짜겠습니다

빛나는 얼굴 눈부시어
고개 숙이면
속으로 타서 익는 까만 꽃씨
당신께 바치는 나의 언어들

이미 하나인 우리가
더욱 하나가 될 날을
확인하고 싶습니다

나의 임금이여
드릴 것은 상처뿐이어도
어둠에 숨지지 않고
섬겨 살기 원이옵니다

A Sunflower's Love Song

As my life is but one,
So is my love.

O my king,
I am upset with the yearning
That pours down like a waterfall.
And it makes me sick of fever unto death.

No one but you can cure me of the fever.
For my love is incurable.

With the yarn spinning from my heart,
I shall weave you
A silk garment from the fine threads.

Before your dazzling face
I bow my head.
And the flower seeds ripen

As burnt within.

They are the words

That I offer you.

I wish to confirm the day

When you and I shall be genuinely one

As we are meant to be.

O my king,

I have nothing to offer you but pain.

Yet, I wish to serve you while living

And not lying dead in the dark.

나비의 연가

가르쳐주시지 않아도
처음부터 알았습니다
나는 당신을 향해 날으는
한 마리 순한 나비인 것을

가볍게 춤추는 나에게도
슬픔의 노란 가루가
남몰래 묻어 있음을 알았습니다

눈멀듯 부신 햇살에
차라리 날개를 접고 싶은
황홀한 은총으로 살아온 나날

빛나는 하늘이
훨훨 날으는
나의 것임을 알았습니다

행복은 가난한 마음임을 가르치는

풀잎들의 합창

수없는 들꽃에게 웃음 가르치며
나는 조용히 타버릴
당신의 나비입니다

부디 꿈꾸며 살게 해주십시오
버려진 꽃들을 잊지 않게 하십시오

들릴 듯 말 듯한 나의 숨결은
당신께 바쳐지는
무언無言의 기도

당신을 향한
맨 처음의 사랑
불망不忘의 나비입니다, 나는

A Butterfly's Love Song

I've come to understand
Without being told that
Since the beginning
I'm a butterfly
Flying toward you.

I've come to understand
I'm secretly stained
With the yellow powder of sorrow
Even as I flitter about.

In the rapture of your grace
I've lived day after day.
In awe I'm tempted to fold my wings
And hide myself from your dazzling rays.

I've come to understand
That the bright sky in which I fly

Was made for me.

I've come to understand
From the choral blades of grass
That happy are the poor in spirit.

Teaching numerous wild flowers to sing
And quietly burning away as designed,
I'm your butterfly.

Grant me to live with dreams
And to remember those
Now decaying flowers.

Even as faint as my breathing sounds
My wordless prayers
Are offered to you.

I'm a butterfly

Never forgetting

My first love is for you.

사랑에 대한 단상

1
나의 사랑에선
늘 송진 향기가 난다

끈적거리지만
싫지 않은
아주 특별한 맛

나는 평생
이 향기를 마시기로 한다
아니 열심히 씹어보기로 한다

2
흔들리긴 해도
쓰러지진 않는
나무와 같이
태풍을 잘 견디어낸

한 그루 나무와 같이

오늘까지
나를 버티게 해준
슬프도록 깊은 사랑이여
고맙고 고마워라

아직도 내 안에서
휘파람을 불며
크고 있는 사랑이여

3
내 마음 안에
이렇듯 깊은 우물 하나
숨어 있는 줄을 몰랐다

네가 나에게

사랑의 말 한마디씩
건네줄 때마다
별이 되어 찰랑이는 물살

어디까지 깊어질지
감당 못하면 어쩌나

Fragmentary Thoughts on Love

1

My love always emits
The aroma of resin.

Sticky, but palatable
Its taste is special.

Throughout my life
I will inhale this aroma
And also chew hard on it.

2

Shaken but never toppled like a mighty oak,
And withstanding the typhoon like a weeping willow,
I have been sustained to this day
By unfathomably deep love.
How very grateful I am!

It is still growing,

Whistling within me.

3

Never had I been aware of such a well,

Hidden within my heart.

Whenever you speak

A word of love to me

It turns into a star

And ripples in my heart.

Even if I am afraid of

The unfathomable depth

As it might be unbearable,

With its beauty

It is ever glorious.

Oh, my well.

봉숭아

한여름 내내
태양을 업고
너만 생각했다

이별도 간절한 기도임을
처음 알았다

어떻게 살아야 할까
어떻게 잊어야 할까

내가 너의 마음 진하게
물들일 수 있다면
네 혼에 불을 놓는
꽃잎일 수 있다면

나는
숨어서도 눈부시게
행복한 거다

A Touch-me-not

Carrying the sun on my back
Throughout the summertime,
I have thought about you.

I have come to know for the first time
That even separation is an earnest prayer.

How should I live?
How should I forget?

I wish I could be a color
That deeply tinges your heart.
And I wish I could be a petal
That enkindles your spirit.

Then, I would be superbly happy
Even if concealed.

석류꽃

지울 수 없는
사랑의 화인火印
가슴에 찍혀

오늘도
달아오른
붉은 석류꽃

황홀하여라
끌 수 없는
사랑

초록의 잎새마다
불을 붙이며
꽃으로 타고 있네

A Pomegranate Blossom

Being possessed,
Its heart is forever marked
With the burning coal of love.

Even today
The pomegranate
Blossoms and glows
Burning within.

What a delightful love it is!
Never quenchable it is.

Igniting each green leaf,
It glows as a flower.

호박꽃

아이를 많이 낳아 키워서
더욱 넉넉하고
따뜻한 마음을 지닌
엄마 같은 꽃

까다롭지 않아 친구가 많은 게야
웬만한 근심 걱정은
다 묻어버린 게야
호들갑을 떨지 않고서도
기쁨을 노래할 줄 아는 꽃

사랑의 꿀 가득 담고
어디든지 뻗어가는
노오란 평화여
순하디순한 용서의 눈빛이여

A Pumpkin Flower

Liberal and warm-hearted as it is,
The flower seems to be a mother
Who has borne and raised many children.

With many a friend,
The flower appears easy to please.
It surely has buried its trivial cares,
And finally has come to sing joyful songs—
Yet, without being overly exuberant.

Stretching wherever desired,
And filled with the honey of love,
The yellow flower reflects genuine peace.
What an amenable forgiving eye it has!

사랑도 나무처럼

사랑도 나무처럼
사계절을 타는 것일까

물오른 설레임이
연둣빛 새싹으로
가슴에 돋아나는
희망의 봄이 있고

태양을 머리에 인 잎새들이
마음껏 쏟아내는 언어들로
누구나 초록의 시인이 되는
눈부신 여름이 있고

열매 하나 얻기 위해
모두를 버리는 아픔으로
눈물겹게 아름다운
충만의 가을이 있고

눈 속에 발을 묻고
홀로 서서 침묵하며 기다리는
인고忍苦의 겨울이 있네

사랑도 나무처럼
그런 것일까

다른 이에겐 들키고 싶지 않은
그리움의 무게를
바람에 실어 보내며
오늘도 태연한 척 눈을 감는
나무여 사랑이여

The Changing Look of Love

Even the look of love changes
With the seasons
Like a tree.

Spring brings hope
With its light green buds
That burst forth in one's heart.

Summer brings a dazzling brilliance
With the sun overhead.
And leaves pour out green words,
Making everybody a poet.

Autumn brings fulfillment
With fruit brought forth
In its extreme beauty
Having painfully forsaken all else.

Winter brings endurance

With silent waiting,

Standing alone

With its feet in the snow.

Doesn't the look of love change

Like a tree?

O my tree, my love,

Pretending to be composed with closed eyes,

Today you secretly cast off

The weight of yearnings

Just as the wind blows.

다른 옷은 입을 수가 없네

'하늘에도
연못이 있네'
소리치다
깨어난 아침

창문을 열고
다시 올려다본 하늘
꿈에 본 하늘이
하도 반가워

나는 그만
그 하늘에 빠지고 말았네

내 몸에 내 혼에
푸른 물이 깊이 들어
이제
다른 옷은
입을 수가 없네

No New Wardrobe

In the morning

I awoke from my sleep, shouting

"There is a lake in the heavens."

Opening the window

I looked up to the heavens.

The same heavens

Seen in my dream

Delighted me.

Oddly,

I have been drawn

Into the heavens.

Having my body and soul tinged deeply

With the azure

I am now moved

Not to get a new wardrobe.

소녀들에게

헤어지고 나면
금방 다시 보고 싶은 그리움으로
너희의 고운 이름을 불러본다

마음이 답답할 때면
죄 없이 맑아서 좋은
너희의 목소리를 그리워하며
하루의 창을 연다

진정 너희가 살아 있어
세상은 아직
향기로운 꽃밭임을 믿으며
희망의 꽃삽을 든다

혼돈과 불안의 시대를 살면서
자주 믿음이 흔들리다가도
너희를 생각하면
마음이 든든하고 부드러워진단다

작은 일에도 감동하고 눈물 흘릴 줄 아는
따뜻함을 다시 배운단다
아직은 어둠을 모르는
그 밝은 웃음과 순결한 눈빛으로
부디 우리에게 힘이 되어다오

지혜와 성실의 기름으로
등불을 밝히고 우리를 이끄는
작은 길잡이가 되어다오
진리를 향한 발걸음을 멈추지 말고
마침내는 선이 승리하는
아름다운 세상을 열어가는
푸른 힘이 되어다오

사랑하는 소녀들아
밤하늘의 별들처럼
먼 데서도 우리를 비추어주는 너희
항상 꿈을 잃지 않는 너희가 있어

오늘도 기쁘단다, 우리는
새롭게 길을 간단다, 우리는

To the Girls

Separated,

And longing to see you again,

We call your lovely names.

Whenever feeling heavy,

And longing to hear your clear, innocent voices,

We open the window to another day.

Believing the world will remain

As a fragrant flower garden,

All the days of your genuine lives,

We take up your spades of hope.

Living in an age of chaos and insecurity,

We have faith but often falter.

Still, we feel emboldened and tenderhearted

Because we have you in mind.

And we come to learn again

Of the warmth that moves us to tears
Even for the least thing.
With your bright smiles and innocent eyes
That have not yet known the darkness,
Extend your helping hands to us.

With the oil of wisdom and integrity
Shine your lights
And be the small guideposts that lead us.
Without breaking your stride toward the truth,
Grow green and strong
And inaugurate a beautiful and just world
Wherein goodness is ever victorious.

Beloved girls,
Like stars in the dark sky,
You cast light over us even from afar,
And you remain full of dreams,

So we are delighted

And walk anew.

상사화

아직 한 번도
당신을
직접 뵙진 못했군요

기다림이 얼마나
가슴 아픈 일인가를
기다려보지 못한 이들은
잘 모릅니다

좋아하면서도
만나지 못하고
서로 어긋나는 안타까움을
어긋나보지 않은 이들은
잘 모릅니다

날마다 그리움으로 길어진 꽃술
내 분홍빛 애틋한 사랑은
언제까지 홀로여야 할까요?

오랜 세월
침묵 속에서
나는 당신께 말하는 법을 배웠고
어둠 속에서
위로 없이도 신뢰하는 법을
익혀왔습니다

죽어서라도 꼭
당신을 만나야지요
사랑은 죽음보다 강함을
오늘은 어제보다
더욱 믿으니까요

A Lovesick Flower*

We haven't met before,
Have we?

How heartbreaking it is to wait!
Those who have not suffered from waiting
Can hardly understand it.

How fretful it is to simply run counter
To someone you're smitten by
And never meet.
Those who've never run counter to one another
Can hardly understand it

Craving you day after day,
My stamens grow ever longer.
How long shall my ardent love
Remain unrequited?

In silence,

Have I learned

How to talk to you.

And in darkness,

Have I learned

How to trust in you

Without being comforted.

Even after death,

I shall meet you.

For more powerful than death is love.

Much more do I believe this today

Than I did yesterday.

---

* *Lycoris squamigera* (Resurrection Lily) – so called because of the flower spikes that appear in late summer long after the leaves disappear. Legend has it that a Buddhist monk fell in love with a beautiful woman while begging for alms in the city. As a monk and unable to actualize that love, he planted this flower to ever remind himself of her and the love that could never be.

파도의 말

울고 싶어도
못 우는 너를 위해
내가 대신 울어줄게
마음 놓고 울어줄게

오랜 나날
네가 그토록
사랑하고 사랑받은
모든 기억들
행복했던 순간들

푸르게 푸르게
내가 대신 노래해줄게

일상이 메마르고
무디어질 땐
새로움의 포말로
무작정 달려올게

A Wave Speaks

Though you want to cry
You cannot.
For your sake, then I will cry
Till my heart is quieted.

You remember all the things
And blessed moments
You have loved
And through which you have been loved
In all the days gone by.

For your sake, then I will sing
A song of the azure and
A song of the deep blue.

I will run to you recklessly
As a foamy balm of newness
For your dull dry routine.

석류의 말

감추려고
감추려고
애를 쓰는데도

어느새
살짝 비어져나오는
이 붉은 그리움은
제 탓이 아니에요

푸름으로
눈부신
가을 하늘 아래

가만히 서 있는 것만으로도
너무 행복해서
터질 것 같은 가슴

이젠 부끄러워도

할 수 없네요

아직은
시고 떫은 채로
그대를 향해
터질 수밖에 없는

이 한 번의 사랑을
부디 아름답다고
말해주어요

A Pomegranate's Words

Though fervently trying to conceal itself
Unnoticeably the red yearning
Stealthily buds forth.
That is not my decision.

Under an autumn sky
Dazzling with the azure—
Even standing still
I am so happy
That my heart seems to swell.

Abashed as I am
I cannot help but burst toward you
Although I am still astringent.

Tell me, please,
"Your love is beautiful."

동백꽃이 질 때

비에 젖은 동백꽃이
바다를 안고
종일토록 토해내는
처절한 울음소리
들어보셨어요?

피 흘려도
사랑은 찬란한 것이라고
순간마다 외치며 꽃을 피워냈듯이
이제는 온몸으로 노래하며
떨어지는 꽃잎들

사랑하면서도
상처를 거부하고
편히 살고 싶은 나의 생각들
쌓이고 쌓이면
죄가 될 것 같아서

마침내 여기
섬에 이르러 행복하네요
동백꽃 지고 나면
내가 그대로
붉게 타오르는 꽃이 되려는
남쪽의 동백섬에서……

When a Camellia Falls

Have you ever heard
A rain-moistened camellia
Embracing the sea
Crying bitterly all day long?

Bleeding, while blooming
The camellia cries at each moment
"Love is brilliant."
Now its petals,
Singing with their whole bodies,
Fall off.

Even in love,
Denying its pains,
I seek a comfortable life.
And thoughts thereof seem sinful
As they pile up,

Finally, having arrived here at the island,

I am so happy.

After the camellia bloom falls

I will become a flower myself

And remain ablaze

On the southern Camellia Island.

찔레꽃

아프다 아프다 하고
아무리 외쳐도

괜찮다 괜찮다 하며
마구 꺾으려는 손길 때문에

나의 상처는
가시가 되었습니다

오랜 세월 남모르게
내가 쏟은
하얀 피
하얀 눈물
한데 모여
향기가 되었다고

사랑은 원래
아픈 것이라고

당신이 내게 말하는 순간

나의 삶은
누구와도 바꿀 수 없는 축복으로
다시 태어났습니다

A White Wild Rose

"Ouch, ouch!"
I painfully cry.

"That's OK. No problem,"
Folks thoughtlessly pluck.

So I gather hurts
That have grown as thorns.

All the silvery tears and blood
I have shed over countless years
Have gathered together
And turned into a fragrance.

At the very moment
I heard you say
"Love is originally painful."
I was born anew—

Into a life ever blessed

And never exchangeable for another.

고독
LONELINESS

―――

숲속의 호수처럼 고요한 마음을 지니게 해주십사고 기도합니다.

시끄럽고 복잡하게 바삐 돌아가는 숨찬 나날들에도

방해를 받지 않고 중심을 잡을 수 있는

마음의 고요를 키우고 싶습니다.

바쁜 것을 핑계로 자주 들여다보지 못해

왠지 낯설고 서먹해진 제 자신과도 화해할 수 있는 고요함,

밖으로 흩어진 마음을 안으로 모아들이는

맑고 깊은 고요함을 지니게 해주십시오.

고요한 기다림 속에 익어가는 고요한 예술로서의 삶을

기대해봅니다.

———

I pray that my heart stays calm like a forest lake. I desire to foster such serenity in the center of a heart freed from the puffy routines and complex noisy rush of life. Using busyness as an excuse, I am rarely reflective. Thus I sometimes feel awkward as well as estranged from my own being. Lord, grant me such a genuine, deep serenity whereby I can reconcile myself with my being, and also collect my mind and heart within, which have been scattered without. I patiently await the consummation of the art of serenity.

11월에

나뭇잎에 지는 세월
고향은 가까이 있고
나의 모습 더없이
초라함을 깨달았네

푸른 계절 보내고
돌아와 묵도하는
생각의 나무여

영혼의 책갈피에
소중히 끼운 잎새
하나 하나 연륜 헤며
슬픔의 눈부심을 긍정하는 오후

햇빛에 실리어오는
행복의 물방울 튕기며
어디론지 떠나고 싶다

조용히 겨울을 넘겨보는
11월의 나무 위에
연처럼 걸려 있는
남은 이야기 하나

지금 아닌
머언 훗날

넓은 하늘가에
너울대는
나비가 될 수 있을까

별밭에 꽃밭에
나뭇잎 지는 세월

나의 원은 너무 커서
차라리 갈대처럼
여위어간다

In November

Now, when the leaves fall,
I see my home nearby,
And see myself as wretched.

You, O tree,
Sending the green season off
And returning to pray silently,
Are ever thoughtful.

Counting the years of leaves
Treasured in my soul's book as bookmarks
I see my sorrow
Turning affirmative this afternoon
And glowing.

I wish to splash in the water drops of happiness
That come to me riding on a sunbeam,
And I wish to leave for someplace.

I have a word that appears like a kite

Hanging on the November tree

And that quietly peeks at the approaching winter.

Not now, but in the distant future,

Can I be a butterfly

And flutter about the vast sky?

Now is the time

That the leaves fall

On the starry and flowery fields.

The circle I draw is so big

That it is stretched ever thinner

Like a reed.

진달래

해마다 부활하는
사랑의 진한 빛깔 진달래여

네 가느단 꽃술이 바람에 떠는 날
상처 입은 나비의 눈매를 본 적이 있니
견딜 길 없는 그리움의 끝을
너는 보았니

봄마다 앓아 눕는
우리들의 지병持病은 사랑

아무것도 보이지 않는다
아무것도 잡히지 않는다

한 점 흰 구름 스쳐 가는 나의 창가에
왜 사랑의 빛은 이토록 선연한가

모질게 먹은 마음도

해 아래 부서지는 꽃가루인데

물이 피 되어 흐르는가
오늘도 다시 피는
눈물의 진한 빛깔 진달래여

O Azalea

Embodied in love's deep colors,
You, O azalea, are raised again
Year after year.

As your thin pistils and stamens
Tremble in the wind,
Have you ever seen the eyes
Of an injured butterfly
And the end of the unbearable longing?

Whenever spring comes,
Ever bedridden are we
With the chronic disease of love.

Nothing is visible.
And nothing is tangible.

Why is the color of love

So vivid at my window
Where a piece of white cloud
Passes by?

Die-hard as my mind is,
It is but pollen
That crumbles under the sun.

Today, in the deep colors
You tearfully bloom again
And flow down like water.
You are as red as blood.

파도여 당신은

파도여 당신은
누워서도 잠들지 않는
바람의 집인가

어느 날 죽어버린
나의 꿈을 일으키며
산이 되는 파도여

오늘도 나는
말을 잃는다

신神의 모습을 닮아
출렁이는 당신이
그리 또한 태연한가

사랑하지 않고는
잠시도 못 견디는
시퍼런 고뇌의 당신이

언젠가 통째로 나를 안을 하느님
파도여 당신은
누워서도 잠 못 드는 기다림인가

You, O Wave

Are you a home
For the never sleeping wind
When you're placid?

You, O wave,
You rise up like a mountain
And raise up my once dead
Dreams to life.

Even today
I'm dumb-founded.

Even while stirred up,
You reflect the serene countenance of God.

Even in the deepest agony
You are compelled
To love unceasingly.

O wave,

Though placid

Will you someday rise,

And enfold me in your bosom

As if you were my God?

사랑

문 닫아도 소용없네
그의 포로 된 후
편히 쉴 날 하루도 없네

아무도 밟지 않은
내 가슴 겨울 눈밭
동백꽃 피 흘리는
아픔이었네

그가 처음으로 내게 왔을 제
나는 이미
그의 것이었네

부르면 빛이 되는
절대의 그
문 닫아도 들어오네

탱자꽃 하얗게

가시 속에 뿜어낸
눈물이었네

Love

Since becoming enchanted by him,
I can't keep him from entering.
So my heart is ever troubled.

On the virgin snow field
Within my heart
I have come to bear pains—
As camellias bleed while flowering.

Unconsciously,
I became possessed by him
Ever since he first came to me.

As I call upon him,
He, the Absolute, turns into light
And enters my hiding place
Even though the door is closed.

The encounter is tearful,

Like the tears white trifoliate flowers shed

Amongst thorns.

바람이여

살 속 깊이 들어박힌
나의 슬픔은
바람이여 모두가 너의 탓이다

바위 끝에 부서지는 이승의 파도 위에
나를 낳아 키워서
갖고 싶은 바람이여

처음의 네 사랑이 칼로 꽂힌 심장에
위로의 눈짓 한번 건네주지 않는
무정한 바람이여

어둠을 일으킨 그대
화살을 쏘아
시름시름 앓아 누운
내 불면의 세월

상처받은 사랑은

할 말이 없다

잠시도 날 잊지 못해
스러진 남은 목숨
불고 싶은 바람이여
죽지 않는 바람이여

You, O Wind

Only you, O wind, cause my sorrows
To deeply embed within me.

Wishing to bear and raise me
On the waves
That break at the edge of the rocks,
You long to possess me.

Since you pierced my heart
With the sword of your first love,
Never have you tried to comfort me
Not even with the glint of an eye.
How cold-hearted you are!

You stirred up the darkness.
And then, you shot the arrow at me
That has caused the lingering illness
From which I've long suffered

Sleeplessly.

No word is found
For the broken love
To voice.

You cannot forget me
For even a moment,
And while still living,
You long to blow.
You, O wind, never die
While vanishing.

나무의 마음으로

참회의 눈물로 뿌리를 내려
하늘과 화해하는
나무의 마음으로 선다

천만 번을 가져도 내가 늘 목마를 당신
보고 싶으면
미루나무 끝에 앉은
겨울바람으로 내가 운다

당신이 빛일수록
더 짙은 어둠인 나
이 세상 누구와도 닮은 일 없는
폭풍 같은 당신을 알아 편할 길 없다

오늘은 엇갈리는 만남의 비극 속에
내일은 열리는가
땅 위의 누구와도 바꿀 수 없는
내 존재의 끝은 당신

편히 잠들 날 없는
가장 정직한 나무의 마음으로
당신 앞에 선다

With a Tree's Heart

I stand erect
With a tree's heart
That reconciles with the heavens
Taking root in tearful contrition.

Even if possessing you
Thousands of times over,
I am ever thirsty for you,
So I sit on the edge of the poplar's bough
Like the winter wind
And weep.

The brighter you shine,
The darker I turn.
I've come to know you—
Appearing stormy
And resembling no one else,
I never feel comfortable but uneasy.

Our crisscrossing paths today
Make for a tragic encounter.
I wish for a clear path tomorrow.
You are the end of my being,
And replaceable by no other.

I stand before you
With a most honest tree's heart
That never allows me
A peaceful night's sleep.

나목 일기

살점을 떼어내는
한밤의 설풍雪風에
내가 앓고 있다

이 목마른 줄기를 축여줄
고운 손길은 없는가

낯익은 사계와의 이별에
해마다 뻗어가는
의지의 뿌리

하늘로 치솟는 고독을
땅 깊이 묻고
황량한 어둠의 들판에 빈 손을 들어
수신인 없는 편지를 쓴다

말로는 풀지 못할
끝없는 사유에

잠 못 드는 겨울

얼어붙은 심장에 불씨를 당길
산새 같은 마음의
친구를 기다린다

A Naked Tree's Diary

In the bitter cold snowstorm
At midnight
Am I afflicted.

Since separation from the familiar seasons,
The root of my will has spread farther
Year after year.

Why can't I have a fair hand
That will offer a drink
To moisten this thirsty stem?

Into the deep earth
Burying my loneliness
That soars toward the heavens,
And to the desolate dark field
Without an addressee
I write a letter

Empty-handed.

Endlessly reflecting on the indescribable,
Hardly can I fall asleep
In this wintertime.

I wait for my friend
Who comes to thaw my frozen heart
With a burning ember
From a mountain bird.

선인장

사막에서도
나를
살게 하셨습니다

쓰디쓴 목마름도
필요한 양식으로
주셨습니다

내 푸른 살을
고통의 가시들로
축복하신 당신

피 묻은
인고의 세월
견딜힘도 주셨습니다

그리하여
살아 있는

그 어느 날

가장 긴 가시 끝에
가장 화려한 꽃 한 송이
피워 물게 하셨습니다

O Cactus

You permit me to live

Even in the desert.

Even the bitter thirst

You grant me

For my nourishment.

You bless my green flesh

With painful thorns.

You strengthen me

To endure times

Of bloody affliction.

In the end,

On a certain day while I live,

You cause me to hold

A most gorgeous flower

At the tip of my longest spine.

비 오는 날의 일기

1
비 오는 날은
촛불을 밝히고
그대에게 편지를 쓰네

습관적으로 내리면서도
습관적인 것을 거부하며
창문을 두드리는 빗소리

그대에게
내가 처음으로 쓰고 싶던
사랑의 말도
부드럽고 영롱한 빗방울로
내 가슴에 다시 파문을 일으키네

2
빨랫줄에 매달린

작은 빗방울 하나
사라지며 내게 속삭이네
혼자만의 기쁨
혼자만의 아픔은
소리로 표현하는 순간부터
상처를 받게 된다고
늘 잠잠히 있는 것이 제일 좋으니
건성으로 듣지 말고 명심하라고
떠나면서 일러주네

3
너무 목이 말라 죽어가던
우리의 산하
부스럼난 논바닥에
부활의 아침처럼
오늘은 하얀 비가 내리네

어떠한 음악보다
아름다운 소리로
산에 들에
가슴에 꽂히는 비
얇디얇은 옷을 입어
부끄러워하는 단비
차갑지만 사랑스런 그 뺨에
입맞추고 싶네

우리도 오늘은
비가 되자

사랑 없어 거칠고
용서 못해 갈라진
사나운 눈길 거두고
이 세상 어디든지
한 방울의 기쁨으로
한 줄기의 웃음으로

순하게 녹아내리는
하얀 비, 고운 비
맑은 비가 되자

4
집도
몸도
마음도
물에 젖어
무겁다

무거울수록
힘든 삶

죽어서도
젖고 싶진 않다고
나의 뼈는

처음으로 외친다

함께 있을 땐
무심히 보아 넘긴
한 줄기 햇볕을
이토록 어여쁜 그리움으로
노래하게 될 줄이야
내 몸과 마음을
퉁퉁 붓게 한 물기를 빼고
어서 가벼워지고 싶다
뽀송뽀송 빛나는 마른 노래를
해 아래 부르고 싶다

A Rainy Day's Diary

1

On a rainy day,

By a burning candle,

I write you a letter.

As the raindrops customarily fall

Yet, denying things routine

I hear them knocking on the window.

Turned into tender crystalline raindrops,

Those words of my love

I wished to write you

Ripple again in my heart.

2

Evaporating,

A raindrop hanging on the clothesline

Suggestively whispers to me,
"From the moment your voice
Expresses your solitary joy
As well as your solitary pain,
You only will be pained.
So staying calm is the best way.
Don't ignore my words
Just keep them in your mind."

3
With mountains and rivers
Once parched and scorched,
Our rice-paddies swelled like boils.
Today, silvery rain falls
As if Easter morning.

Embedding itself in the mountains and rivers

And in my heart as well,

The falling rain sounds more beautiful

Than any other music.

So flimsily dressed,

The refreshing rain appears abashed.

I wish to kiss its chilly but lovely cheeks.

Turning away from hostile eyes

That are harsh, loveless and unforgiving—

Eyes that cut and divide,

Shall we be like the rain today?

Shall we become a fine, clear, silver rain?

And, then, we will softly fall everywhere

Thawing the world

As drops of joy

And as streams of laughter.

4

Drenched in the rainfall,

My shelter, my body,

And my mind—

All are heavy.

The heavier they grow,

The harder my life becomes.

"Even dead,

We don't want to be drenched,"

My bones are first to scream.

When I was with someone else,

Unconsciously, I paid little attention

To the beaming sunshine.

Now, amazingly,

I crave and sing to it.

Thoroughly damp as my body and mind are,
I desire to be quickly dried and lightened
And to sing a dry but splendid song
Under the sun.

장미를 생각하며

우울한 날은
장미 한 송이 보고 싶네

장미 앞에서
소리내어 울면
나의 눈물에도 향기가 묻어날까

감당 못할 사랑의 기쁨으로
내내 앓고 있을 때
나의 눈을 환히 밝혀주던 장미를
잊지 못하네

내가 물 주고 가꾼 시간들이
겹겹의 무늬로 익어 있는 꽃잎들 사이로
길이 열리네

가시에 찔려 더욱 향기로웠던
나의 삶이

암호처럼 찍혀 있는
아름다운 장미 한 송이
'살아야 해, 살아야 해'
오늘도 내 마음에
불을 붙이네

Reflecting on a Rose

On a sullen day,
I desire to see a rose.

Wailing before the rose,
I wonder if its fragrance
Can blend with my tears.

Hardly can I forget the rose
That opened my eyes wide.
With the delight of love
I was unbearably pained.

All the hours
I watered and tended
Have brought forth mature petals.
In the enfolding patterns
I see a pathway open.

Pierced by the thorns,

My life has turned more scented.

And, on the rose

My life is engraved

As a cipher.

Today,

The rose stirs my heart ablaze, saying

"You must live. You must love."

너에게 가겠다

오늘도
한줄기
노래가 되어
너에게 가겠다

바람 속에 떨면서도
꽃은 피어나듯이

사랑이 낳아준
눈물 속에
하도 잘 익어서
별로 뜨는
나의 시간들

침묵할수록
맑아지는 노래를
너는 듣게 되겠지

무게를 견디지 못한
그리움이 흰 모래로
부서지는데

멈출 수 없는
하나의 노래로
나는 오늘도
너에게 달려가겠다

I Will Come to You

Today
Becoming a meter of song,
I will come to you again.

Even trembling in the wind,
A flower blooms.

With tears born of love
My times ripen fully
And rise as the stars.

The longer my silence stretches,
The clearer my song sounds.
And you can hear it.

Heavier and heavier— unbearably so,
My craving shatters
Into silvery grains of sand.

Today

With a song

That I cannot restrain

I will run to you again.

이끼 낀 돌층계에서

이끼 낀 돌층계에
내가 찍어놓은
그리움의 발자국

오늘은 어제보다
조금 더
죽음이 가까워도
세월은 푸르게
나를 안고 있다

층계에서 별을 보면
고요하고 따뜻해라

오늘의 눈물은 모두
이끼 속에 숨기고
환안히 웃어야지

내일을 기다리는

연인이 되어야지

On the Mossy Stone Steps

Tracing my yearnings,
My footprints remain
On the mossy stone steps.

As death draws a little nearer today
Blue-skied times embrace me.

At the steps,
I look up to the stars—
How calm and warm they are!

The moss conceals
All the tears
I shed today—
I wear a bright smile.

I would rather be a lover
Awaiting tomorrow.

사르비아의 노래

저 푸른 가을 하늘
물 같은 서늘함으로
내 사랑의 열도(熱度) 높음을
식히고 싶다

아무리 아름다운 상처라지만
끝내는 감당 못할
사랑의 출혈(出血)
이제는 조금씩
멈추게 하고 싶다

바람아
너는 알겠니?

네 하얀 붕대를 풀어
피투성이의 나를
싸매다오

불 같은 뜨거움으로
한여름을 태우던
나의 꽃심장이
너무도 아프단다, 바람아

A Salvia's Song

With the cool water of the autumnal azure,
I wish to quench
The burning fever of my love.

However sweet the bruise might be,
It is an uncontrollable love that bleeds.
Now, I wish it to go away.

O wind,
You do understand,
Don't you?

Loosen your white bandage,
And, with it,
Firmly bind my bleeding wound.

Scorched by the mid-summer blaze,
So painful has my flower-like heart become.

You, O wind surely understand.

어느 조가비의 노래

바다 어머니
흰 모래밭에 엎디어
모래처럼 부드러운 침묵 속에
그리움을 참고 참아
진주로 키우려고 했습니다

밤낮으로 파도에 밀려온
아픔의 세월 속에
이만큼 비워내고
이만큼 단단해진 제 모습을
자랑스레 보여드리고 싶습니다

아직 못다 이룬 꿈들
못다 한 말들 때문에
슬퍼하거나 애태우지 않으렵니다

행복은 멀리 있지 않으니
가슴속에 고요한 섬 하나 들여놓고

조금씩 기쁨의 별을 키우라고
먼 데서도 일러주시는 푸른 어머니
비어서 더욱 출렁이는 마음에
자꾸 고여오는 넓고 깊은 사랑을
저는 어떻게 감당할까요?

이 세상 하얀 모래밭에 그 사랑을
두고두고 쏟아낼 수밖에 없는
저의 이름은 '작은 기쁨' 조가비
하늘과 바다로 사랑의 편지를 보내는
'흰구름' 조가비입니다

A Shell's Song

Mother-Sea,
In tender silence
Prostrating myself on the silvery sand,
I have patiently sustained my yearning
And desired to bring forth a pearl.

Along with the painful tide and time
That surges every day and night
I have greatly emptied myself
And have become sturdy.

Now I wish to show you
How I have changed.

For those dreams
That have not yet come true
And for those words
Not fully expressed,

I no longer grieve or worry about.

From a distance
You, O Blue Mother, say,
"As your happiness is not afar,
Place a calm island in your heart
And grow thereon a star of joy
Little by little."

Since my heart is emptied,
Therein are more ripples
And it endlessly gathers a big and deep love.
How can I contain it?

In the world
I cannot help but pour out love
Over the silvery field of sand.
As I am a shell named "Small Joy,"

I shall be a shell of the white cloud

That sends a love letter

To the sky, and to the sea as well.

해 질 무렵 어느 날

꽃 지고 난 뒤
바람 속에 홀로 서서
씨를 키우고
씨를 날리는 꽃나무의 빈집

쓸쓸해도 자유로운
그 고요한 웃음으로
평화로운 빈 손으로

나도 모든 이에게
살뜰한 정 나누어주고
그 열매 익기 전에
떠날 수 있을까

만남보다
빨리 오는 이별 앞에
삶은 가끔 눈물겨워도
아름다웠다고 고백하는

해 질 무렵 어느 날

애틋하게 물드는
내 가슴의 노을빛 빈집

At Sunset on a Certain Day

After the flowers fall

The wind blowing through the empty house

Winnows the seeds,

And blows them away.

Free, but lonely,

Wearing a serene smile,

And offering open hands.

Can I share my sincere affection with all people

And then depart before the fruit ripens?

Now, at sunset on a certain day—

Departing even before arriving

I can still confess

Life is sometimes tearful

But beautiful.

And then the evening glow tinges

The empty house within my heart.

기도
PRAYER

살아 있는 동안은 나이에 상관없이
능금처럼 풋풋하고 설레는 마음을 주십사고 기도합니다.
사람과 자연과 사물에 대해 창을 닫지 않는 열린 마음,
삶의 경이로움에 자주 감동할 수 있는
시인의 마음을 지니고 싶습니다.
타성에 젖어 무디고 둔하고 메마른 삶을
적셔줄 수 있는 예리한 감성을
항상 기도로 갈고 닦게 해주십시오.

My lifelong prayer is that, regardless of age, I desire a throbbing, ever-excited heart like a ripening fresh apple. It is a poet's heart that I wish to cherish, one that remains open to people, nature and things alike, often leaping for the wonder of life. With constant prayer, may I have a keen emotion cultivated and refined enough to quicken those lives that have been stereotyped, dulled, numbed and dried out.

장미의 기도

피게 하소서
주여

당신이 주신 땅에
가시덤불 헤치며
피 흘리는 당신을
닮게 하소서

태양과 바람
흙과 빗줄기에
고마움 새롭히며
피어나게 하소서

내 뾰족한 가시들이 남에게
큰 아픔 되지 않게 하시며
나를 위한 고뇌 속에
성숙하는 기쁨을
알게 하소서

주여
당신 한 분
믿고
사랑하게 하소서

오직 당신만을 위해
마음 가다듬는
슬기를
깨우치게 하소서

진정
살아 있는 동안은
피 흘리게 하소서
죽어서 다시 피는
목숨이게 하소서

A Rose's Prayer

O Lord,
Help me bloom.

In the land
Where Thou has planted me,
May I imitate Thee
Who bled pushing through the brambles.

With the sun, wind, earth
And rainshowers
May I renew my gratitude
And bloom.

May my prickly thorns
Never cause others big pains,
But may I remain aware of the joy
That painfully mellows me.

O Lord,

May I love

And trust Thee only.

May I be enlightened

With wisdom

To brace my mind

For Thee only.

Surely,

As long as I live,

May I offer my blood

That I may lead such a life

To bloom again

After death.

다시 바다에서

열여섯 살에 처음으로
환희의 눈물 속에
내가 만났던 바다

짜디짠 소금물로
나의 부패를 막고
내가 잠든 밤에도
파도로 밀려와
작고 좁은 내 영혼의 그릇을
어머니로 채워주던 바다

침묵으로 출렁이는
그 속 깊은 말
수평선으로 이어지는 기도를
오늘도 다시 듣네

낮게 누워서도
높은 하늘 가득 담아

하늘의 편지를 읽어주며
한 순간도 놓치지 않고
내게 영원을 약속하는 바다
푸른 사제 푸른 시인을
나는 죽어서도
잊을 수 없네

At the Sea Again

When I was sixteen
I met the sea for the first time
With tears of joy.

With its salty water
The sea kept me from decaying
And filled my small soul
As did my mother
With waves coming to me at night
Even while I slept.

Today I hear again the profound words
Of waves silently moving as prayers
Binding me to the horizon.

Even lying low
And fully containing the high sky,
The sea, without even pausing for an instant,

Reads the heavenly letter to me

And promises me eternity.

Thus, the blue sea becomes

Both priest and poet,

Unforgettable

Even unto my death.

한 송이 수련으로

내가 꿈을 긷는 당신의 못 속에
하얗게 떠다니는
한 송이 수련으로 살게 하소서

겹겹이 쌓인 평생의 그리움
물 위에 풀어놓고
그래도 목말라 물을 마시는 하루

도도한 사랑의 불길조차
담담히 다스리며 떠다니는
당신의 꽃으로 살게 하소서

밤마다
별을 안고 합장하는
물빛의 염원

단 하나의 영롱한 기도를
어둠의 심연에서 건져내게 하소서

나를 위해
순간마다 연못을 펼치는 당신

그 푸른 물 위에
말없이 떠다니는
한 송이 수련으로 살게 하소서

Desiring to be a Water Lily

May I live as a white water lily

Floating on your lake

From whence I draw my dreams.

After spreading the heavy layers

Of lifelong longings

Onto the water,

I am ever thirsty

And drink again today.

May I live as your serene flower

That quenches even the rush

Of blazing love

While floating.

Night after night

I invoke my wish

Of the aquamarine

With my hands joined.

May I draw a single lucid prayer
Out of the dark depths.

Moment by moment
You spread the lake for me.

May I live as a water lily
Floating on the blue water
Without uttering a word.

엉겅퀴의 기도

제가 필요한 곳이면
어디든지 가겠습니다
누구에게든지 가서
벗이 되겠습니다

참을성 있는 기다림과
절제 있는 다스림으로
가시 속에서도 꽃을 피워낸
큰 기쁨을 님께 드리겠습니다

불길을 지난 사랑 속에서만
물 같은 삶의 노래를 부를 수 있음을
내게 처음으로 가르쳐준 당신

모든 걸 당신께 맡기면서도
때로는 불안했고
저 자신의 무게를 감당하기
어려울 때도 많았습니다

일상의 잔잔한 평화와
고운 질서를 거부하고 달아나고 싶던
저의 보랏빛 반란이
너무도 길었음을 용서하십시오

이젠 더 이상
진실을 거부하지 않겠습니다
허영심을 버리고
그대로의 제가 되겠습니다

당신이 원하시는 곳으로
저를 불러주십시오
참회의 눈물을 흘린 후의
가장 겸허한 모습으로
모든 이를 사랑하게 하십시오

A Thistle's Prayer

Wherever I may be wanted,
There will I come.
And to whomever I may come,
A friend will I be.

Waiting with patience
And attuning myself
With temperance,
I will bring you a great joy,
Flowering even among thorns.

You are the one
Who showed me for the first time
That I can sing a song of water-like life
Only by having a love tempered by fire.

Though committed to you
From time to time

I feel insecure.

And often I can hardly bear

Even my own burdens.

Forgive me

For my prolonged violent rebellion.

For I once wanted to run away,

Denying mundane serenity

And genuine order.

No longer

Shall I deny the truth.

And now shall I be

As one freed

From vainglory.

To wherever you may desire,

Call me, please

That I may love all persons

With the lowliest mind

After having shed tears

Of contrition.

꽃밭에 서면

꽃밭에 서면 큰 소리로 꽈리를 불고 싶다
피리를 불듯이
순결한 마음으로

꽈리 속의 자디잔 씨알처럼
내 가슴에 가득 찬 근심 걱정
후련히 쏟아내며
꽈리를 불고 싶다

아무도 미워하지 않는 동그란 마음으로
꽃밭에 서면

저녁노을 바라보며
지는 꽃의 아름다움에
흠뻑 취하고 싶다

남의 잘못을
진심으로 용서하고

나의 잘못을
진심으로 용서받고 싶다
꽃들의 죄 없는 웃음소리
붉게 타오르는
꽃밭에 서면

Standing in the Flower Garden

Standing in the flower garden
I want to blow on an empty ground cherry
With all of my pure heart,
As if playing a reed flute.

I want to blow on the ground cherry,
Casting out all my cares and worries
And thus, refresh my spirit.
For my mind is occupied with them
As a ground cherry is filled
With numerous seeds.

Standing in the flower garden
With an overflowing heart that hates nobody,
I want to gaze at the evening glow
While yet fully captivated by
The beauty of falling leaves.

As I truly forgive those who do me wrong,

So do I want to be forgiven of my wrongdoings.

Standing in the glowing flower garden,

I hear the innocent laughter of the flowers.

제비꽃 연가

나를 받아주십시오

헤프지 않은 나의 웃음
아껴둔 나의 향기
모두 당신의 것입니다

당신이 가까이 오셔야
나는 겨우 고개를 들어
웃을 수 있고
감추어진 향기도
향기인 것을 압니다

당신이 가까이 오셔야
내 작은 가슴속엔
하늘이 출렁일 수 있고
내가 앉은 이 세상은
아름다운 집이 됩니다

담담한 세월을
뜨겁게 안고 사는 나는
가장 작은 꽃이지만
가장 큰 기쁨을 키워드리는
사랑꽃이 되겠습니다

당신의 삶을
온통 봄빛으로 채우기 위해
어둠 밑으로 뿌리내린 나
비 오는 날에도 노래를 멈추지 않는
작은 시인이 되겠습니다

나를 받아주십시오

A Violet's Love Song

Accept me as I am:

For my laughter restrained
And my fragrance preserved
Are all yours.

If you come close to me
I may burst into joyous laughter.
Barely raising my head
The heretofore masked
True fragrance is revealed.

If you come close to me
I may even have the sky
Ripple in my small heart
And the earth I'm standing on
Turn into a splendid mansion.

Even as the least among the flowers
And fervently embracing these ordinary days,
I shall be a flower of love
Fostering your greatest joy.

Rooted in the dark soil
Solely to fill your life
With the color of spring,
I shall be like a humble poet
Endlessly composing
Even on the rainiest days.

Accept me as I am.

겨울 아가 1

눈보라 속에서 기침하는
벙어리 겨울나무처럼
그대를 사랑하리라

밖으로는 눈꽃을
안으로는 뜨거운 지혜의 꽃 피우며
기다림의 긴 추위를 이겨내리라

비록 어느 날
눈사태에 쓰러져
하얀 피 흘리는
무명無名의 순교자가 될지라도
후회 없는 사랑의 아픔
연약한 나의 두 팔로
힘껏 받아 안으리라

모든 잎새의 무게를 내려놓고
하얀 뼈 마디 마디 봄을 키우는

겨울나무여

나도 언젠가는
끝없는 그리움의 무게를
땅 위에 내려놓고 떠나리라

노래하며 노래하며
순백純白의 눈사람으로
그대가 나를 기다리는
순백의 나라로

Winter Song of Songs 1

I shall love you

As a mute winter tree

Coughing in a blizzard.

I shall endure

The long days of expectation,

Turning snow without into wintry beauty

And wisdom within into warmth.

Though I may be an unknown martyr someday

Pouring out pure blood

And lying fallen by a snowslide,

I shall hold the pain of love

In my feeble arms without regret.

O winter tree,

You nourish the spring in each fork

Unlading the weight of all your leaves.

So shall I leave someday—

Unlading the weight of my endless yearnings

On earth.

Thus, I shall come to the country

Where you, as a pure snowman,

Wait for me

With continuous singing.

가난한 새의 기도

꼭 필요한 만큼만 먹고
필요한 만큼만 둥지를 틀며
욕심을 부리지 않는 새처럼
당신의 하늘을 날게 해주십시오

가진 것 없어도
맑고 밝은 웃음으로
기쁨의 깃을 치며
오늘을 살게 해주십시오

예측할 수 없는 위험을 무릅쓰고
먼 길을 떠나는 철새의 당당함으로
텅 빈 하늘을 나는
고독과 자유를 맛보게 해주십시오

오직 사랑 하나로
눈물 속에도 기쁨이 넘쳐날
서원의 삶에

햇살로 넘쳐오는 축복

나의 선택은
가난을 위한 가난이 아니라
사랑을 위한 가난이기에
모든 것 버리고도
넉넉할 수 있음이니

내 삶의 하늘에 떠다니는
흰 구름의 평화여

날마다 새가 되어
새로이 떠나려는 내게
더 이상
무게가 주는 슬픔은 없습니다

A Poor Bird's Prayer

As a bird eats only as much as needed
And makes a nest only as big as needed,
Make me fly in your sky freed from greed.

Possessing nothing
But wearing a clear, bright smile
And preening feathers of joy,
May I live today.

As a migrating bird boldly starts
On a long journey,
Enduring unknown dangers,
May I taste the solitude
And freedom of the empty sky.

With love only,
Even amidst tears
The beaming sun

Richly, joyfully blesses
My professed life.

With poverty chosen
Not for its own sake
But for the sake of love
I am now rich,
Having forsaken all.

Oh, what peaceful white clouds
Float in the sky of my life!

Day by day
I wish to be a bird
And start anew
Unburdened.

눈꽃 아가

1
차갑고도 따스하게
송이송이 시가 되어 내리는 눈
눈나라의 흰 평화는 눈이 부셔라

털어내면 그뿐
다신 달라붙지 않는
깨끗한 자유로움

가볍게 쌓여서
조용히 이루어내는
무게와 깊이

하얀 고집을 꺾고
끝내는 녹아버릴 줄도 아는
온유함이여

나도 그런 사랑을 해야겠네

그대가 하얀 눈사람으로
나를 기다리는 눈나라에서
하얗게 피어날 줄밖에 모르는
눈꽃처럼 그렇게 단순하고
순결한 사랑을 해야겠네

2
평생을 오들오들
떨기만 해서 가여웠던
해묵은 그리움도
포근히 눈밭에 눕혀놓고
하늘을 보고 싶네

어느 날 내가
지상의 모든 것과 작별하는 날도
눈이 내리면 좋으리

하얀 눈 속에 길게 누워
오래도록 사랑했던
신과 이웃을 위해
이기심의 짠맛은 다 빠진
맑고 투명한 물이 되어 흐를까

녹지 않는 꿈들일랑 얼음으로 남기고
누워서도 잠 못 드는
하얀 침묵으로 깨어 있을까

3
첫눈 위에
첫 그리움으로
내가 써보는 네 이름

맑고 순한 눈빛의 새 한 마리
나뭇가지에서 기침하며

나를 내려다본다

자꾸 쌓이는 눈 속에
네 이름은 고이 묻히고
사랑한다, 사랑한다
무수히 피어나는 눈꽃 속에

나 혼자 감당 못할
사랑의 말들은
내 가슴속으로 녹아 흐르고
나는 그대로
하얀 눈물이 되려는데

누구에게도 말 못할
한 방울의 피와 같은 아픔도
눈밭에 다 쏟아놓고 가라

부리 고운 저 분홍가슴의 새는

자꾸 나를 재촉하고……

Snow Flower Songs

1

It's snowing, falling in flakes
And each flake is turning into
A cold but warm poem.
How dazzling is the white peace
In the snow country!

Once shaken off
Never do they again stick together.
How clean and free they are!

Softly piling up,
Quietly they grow complete.
How heavy and deep they are!

Breaking their white stubbornness
They eventually melt.
How meek they are!

So should I love you

As the snowman you are

In the snow country

Where you wait for me.

As a snow flower blooms in white only

So pure and simple

Shall my love be.

2

Shivering throughout my life

I now wish to tenderly lay

My pitiful yearnings of long years

On the snow field

And to gaze up to the sky.

Someday when I depart from earth,
Bidding farewell to all,
I wish it to be a snowy day
And to lie full length in the snow.

For God and my neighbors
Whom I have long loved
I shall melt away as crystal clear water
Freed from my salty egoism.

Leaving those dreams frozen as ice
And unable to sleep,
I stay awake in the white silence.

3
In the first snow
Yearning for you,

I write your name.

With clear and tender eyes
A bird on the bough,
Gazing down on me,
Coughs.

Under the snow piling up
Your name is gently buried,
And in the countless snow flowers
My love for you will always remain.
I love you.

Those words of love
Unbearable by myself alone
Thawed, flow in my heart.
I too wish to become white tears.

And your blood-like pain
Is unspeakable to anyone.
Pour it out on the snowy field
And depart.

The robin redbreast with pretty beak
Quickens me again.

봄까치꽃

까치가 놀러 나온
잔디밭 옆에서

가만히 나를 부르는
봄까치꽃

하도 작아서
눈에 먼저 띄는 꽃

어디 숨어 있었니?
언제 피었니?

반가워서 큰 소리로
내가 말을 건네면

어떻게 대답할까
부끄러워
하늘색 얼굴이

더 얇아지는 꽃

잊었던 네 이름을 찾아
내가 기뻤던 봄

노래처럼 다시 불러보는
너, 봄까치꽃

잊혀져도 변함 없이
제자리를 지키며
나도 너처럼
그렇게 살면 좋겠네

A Magpie Flower in Spring

Standing by the lawn,
Where a magpie comes to play,
A magpie flower calmly beckons me.

Small as the flower is,
I spot it immediately.

Where did you hide?
When did you bloom?

Excited,
I try to talk to it aloud,
Breaking the ice.

Embarrassed,
Knowing not how to respond,
The flower's blue face
Softens.

In the springtime,
Recalling your name
Once forgotten,
Ever delightful I am.

As if singing a song,
I beckon you again,
O spring magpie flower.

Even if once forgotten,
You still keep your place
Without changing.
I wish I could live as you do,
O spring magpie flower.

춘분 일기

바람이 불 듯 말 듯
꽃이 필 듯 말 듯

해마다 3월 21일은
파밭의 흙 한 줌 찍어다가
내가 처음으로
시를 쓰는 날입니다

밤과 낮의 길이가
똑같다구요?

모든 이에게
골고루 사랑을 나누어주는
봄햇살 엄마가 되고 싶다고

춘분처럼
밤낮 길이가 똑같아서 공평한
세상의 누이가 되고 싶다고

일기에 썼습니다

아직 겨울이 숨어 있는
꽃샘바람에
설레며 피어나는
내 마음의 춘란 한 송이

오늘따라
은은하고
어여쁩니다

Diary on the Vernal Equinox

It looks windy,
And the flower looks as if blooming.

Every year
On the twenty-first of March
Taking a handful of soil
From the onion patch,
I write my first letter.

Both day and night
Are of equal length
Aren't they?

I wish I were mother of the sunshine
 Whereby my love is distributed fairly to all.
 And I wish I were a sister of a fair world
 Wherein day and night are equally long
 Like today.

With these words

I write today's diary.

In my heart

A spring orchid* has come to flower

Throbbing with the spring frost

That contains winter's vestige.

Today,

It looks unusually serene,

And so lovely.

* Cymbidium goeringii

외딴 마을의 빈집이 되고 싶다

나는 문득
외딴 마을의
빈집이 되고 싶다

누군가 이사 오길 기다리며
오랫동안 향기를 묵혀둔
쓸쓸하지만 즐거운 빈집

깔끔하고 단정해도
까다롭지 않아 넉넉하고
하늘과 별이 잘 보이는
한 채의 빈집

어느 날
문을 열고 들어올 주인이
"음, 마음에 드는데……"
하고 나직이 속삭이며 미소 지어줄
깨끗하고 아름다운 빈집이 되고 싶다

Longing to be Empty and Isolated

Suddenly

I long to be an empty house

In an isolated village.

It should be bare and empty

But pleasant,

With a fragrance long preserved,

And waiting for someone to move in.

An empty house

As clean and tidy as it might be,

Yet open and simple,

From whence I can see the sky and the stars.

Someday

Its master will open the door and enter,

Softly saying, with a smile, "Oh, I really like it."

It is as clean and lovely as the master desires.

작은 위로

잔디밭에 쓰러진
분홍색 상사화를 보며
혼자서 울었어요

쓰러진 꽃들을
어떻게
위로해야 할지 몰라
하늘을 봅니다

비에 젖은 꽃들도
위로해주시구요
아름다운 죄가 많아
가엾은 사람들도
더 많이 사랑해주세요

보고 싶은 하느님
오늘도 하루 종일
꼼짝을 못하겠으니

어서 저를
일으켜주십시오
지혜의 웃음으로
저를 적셔주십시오

Small Comfort

Seeing pink lovesick flowers*
Lying fallen on the green grass,
I weep alone.

Knowing not how to comfort
Those fallen flowers,
I gaze up to the sky.

Comfort, please, those rain-soaked flowers,
And love the pitiful souls
For they have only committed beautiful sins.

God, I miss you.
Today, all day long,
I can't budge.

So raise me up quickly
And infuse me

With your wise smile.

* See p.138

능소화 연가

이렇게
바람 많이 부는 날은
당신이 보고 싶어
내 마음이 흔들립니다

옆에 있는 나무들에게
실례가 되는 줄 알면서도
나도 모르게
가지를 뻗은 그리움이
자꾸자꾸 올라갑니다

저를 다스릴 힘도
당신이 주실 줄 믿습니다

다른 사람들이 내게 주는
찬미의 말보다
침묵 속에도 불타는
당신의 그 눈길 하나가

나에겐 기도입니다
전 생애를 건 사랑입니다

A Trumpet Vine's Love Song

Missing you
On a day like today,
My heart quivers.

Although rude to neighboring trees,
I unconsciously climb higher and higher
As my yearning tendrils reach out
Ceaselessly.

I believe
You will fortify me enough
To control myself.

Rather than words of praise from others,
It is your silently burning eyes
That inspire my prayers,
And it is love
Whereon my entire life hangs.

아침의 향기

아침마다
소나무 향기에
잠이 깨어
창문을 열고
기도합니다

오늘 하루도
솔잎처럼 예리한 지혜와
푸른 향기로
나의 사랑이
변함 없기를

찬물에 세수하다 말고
비누향기 속에 풀리는
나의 아침에게
인사합니다

오늘 하루도

온유하게 녹아서
누군가에게 향기를 묻히는
정다운 벗이기를
평화의 노래이기를

The Fragrance of Morning

Every morning
I open the window.
I'm awakened by the fragrance of pine,
And I pray.

Today
My love may remain unchanged
As a pine needle is
With its sharp wisdom
And green fragrance.

While washing my face with cold water,
Holding my breath,
I greet the morn
That dissolves with the scent of soap.

Today
I may dissolve meekly,

Emitting fragrance

As an affectionate friend

And a song of peace.

SNOW FLOWER SONGS

First published in 2005 by Yolimwon Publishing Co.

Yolimwon Publishing Co.
152, Hoedong-gil, Paju-si, Gyeonggi-do, 10881, Korea
www.yolimwon.com

Copyright © Claudia Hae In Lee, 2005, 2025
English Translation Copyright © Jinsup Kim, 2005, 2025

All rights reserved. No part of this translation may be reproduced or transmitted in any form, or by any means, electronic or mechanical, including photocopying, recording, taping, or any information storage and retrieval system, without permission in writing from the publisher or the translator, except by a reviewer who may quote brief passages in a review.

눈꽃 아가

초 판 1쇄 발행 2005년 10월 25일
개정판 1쇄 발행 2025년 7월 15일

지은이 이해인
옮긴이 김진섭·유진 W. 자일펠더
주간 김종숙 | 기획실 정진우 정재우
편집 김은혜 정소영 김혜원
디자인 강희철 | 마케팅 홍보 고다희
디지털콘텐츠 구지영 | 제작 관리 윤준수 고은정 김선애

펴낸곳 도서출판 열림원 | 펴낸이 정중모
출판등록 1980년 5월 19일(제406-2000-000204호)
주소 경기도 파주시 회동길 152
전화 031-955-0700 | 팩스 031-955-0661
홈페이지 www.yolimwon.com | 이메일 editor@yolimwon.com
페이스북 /yolimwon | 트위터 @yolimwon | 인스타그램 @yolimwon

ISBN 979-11-7040-339-5 03810

• 저자와 출판사의 서면 허락 없이 내용의 일부를 무단 도용하거나 발췌하는 것을 금합니다.
• 책값은 뒤표지에 있습니다. 잘못된 책은 구입하신 곳에서 교환해드립니다.